Throaty Wipes

Susan Holbrook

Coach House Books, Toronto

Canada Council   Conseil des Arts
for the Arts   du Canada
 ONTARIO ARTS COUNCIL
CONSEIL DES ARTS DE L'ONTARIO
an Ontario government agency
un organisme du gouvernement de l'Ontario
Canadä

Published with the generous assistance of the Canada Council for the
Arts and the Ontario Arts Council. Coach House Books also acknowl-
edges the support of the Government of Canada through the Canada
Book Fund and the Government of Ontario through the Ontario Book
Publishing Tax Credit and the Ontario Book Fund.

LIBRARY AND ARCHIVES CANADA CATALOGUING IN PUBLICATION

Holbrook, Susan L. (Susan Leslie), 1967-, author
     Throaty wipes / Susan Holbrook. -- First edition.

Poems.
ISBN 978-1-55245-328-5 (paperback).

     I. Title.

PS8565.O412T57 2016   C811'.54   C2015-908206-4

Throaty Wipes is available as an ebook: ISBN 978 1 77056 445 9

for Nicole

WHAT IS POETRY

(a twelve-tone poem)

trite yap show
rosy twit heap
posterity haw
a wept history
it's yawp rot, eh
a wisher potty
a power shitty
a whitey sport

poetry is what
whips yo tater
pets it awry, oh
oh, twisty pear
two hearts yip
it's paw theory

hi! try wet soap

ear whist typo
ape with story
or what ye spit
or what yeps it

throaty wipes
or what I types

LAYMAN'S TERMS

Okay, say the tower
is bathwater, the dish
is your drainpipe, your
computer a septic tank,
the trees a cracked
waste shoe. Okay,
the tower is a gas
tank, the dish is a crank-
case, the trees a leaky
fuel injector and your
computer a rough or
hesitant idler. The tower
is your brain, okay? Your
dish is your mouth,
the trees the inhibitory
neurotransmitter gamma-
aminobutyric acid, your
computer slurring, 'This
time make it a double.'
The tower is power,
your computer is a hair
dryer, your dish
a plug, the trees
insulation under the screw.
Trees are a slotted spoon,
okay? The tower is a dish,
your computer a leaky
mouth, your dish
another dish. Say
the tower's a red
fish, your dish

a spawning pool.
Your trees are too
shallow. Your computer
is a cobble riffle, a forest is a pin-
ball machine, a tree is a cotton ball, okay?
Your arms slur and plug,
there are dishes
in the tub. The sun
flash-broils the moon,
but your computer
is Earth under a messy
blue sky of trees.
A viper
appears to chew
the rat, but
in reality it
is toothing in
more venom
so it can swallow
its prey whole okay that's
what you want

MUST WE LEARN THESE THINGS
FOR OURSELVES

The body
rejects surplus
vodka, scab-
dug knees sprout
burls, credit-card debt
never stops interesting,
they shellac the display cakes. Lust
that could flay an Airbus to tinsel, spatter all matter with singe-
holes which dilate rapidly until they meet and the universe
puckers into rope ladders in various states of dissolve, does not
bode well. You can't call
Information to get
information. I needed
the name of that Walter
Crane painting, you know,
where rearing horses
form the foam? Surf,
yes, a weird bronco and
weird is spelt that way.
Spelt spelled that way.
Her warning not to touch
the orange coil at eye
level in the kitchen
of 646 Gordon Street
proved nontheoretical.
Get the fingering right
the first time because
your hands are hands-on
learners and stubborn
elephants. Lopped

lollipop to wind-
pipe as bung is
to bottle, as the shout
not to run and suck's
stuck. Now I get my
information from the Internet.
There's a pamphlet on how to dress
without a corset and
seahorses on the brain
floor, where all
we know
goes.

MY FELLOW CONTRANYM

We overlooked
the ocean, trimming
itself.

I devoured the pitted
plums. You prefer
the pitted kind.

The cookies had
been dusted. Love
garnished.

I was chuffed
but you were
chuffed.

I tabled my
apology. You
tabled your apology.

We agreed
to sanction
aught.

Our transparent
desires cleaved
and buckled.

We overlooked
the ocean, trimming
itself.

Fast ravel.
The alarm went
off. Nobody left.

It's better to use both hands. It's better to leave the hands out of it. It's better to introduce saliva. It's better to encourage it to go left if you want it to fall to the right. Better to cover the hole with your thumb to trap air inside. Better to go for the good old-fashioned pink doughy kind. Better to consider that the emperor and his family cannot partake. Better to let the leaves dry first. Better to make a deeper dimple for the punty, *punty* coming from the French or Italian term for bridge. Better to keep the tongue engaged. Better to think of it as honey on the tip of a butter knife. Better to separate it into three sections, securing with a ponytail holder. Better to keep the wind at your back. Better to avoid larger ones, which will cause problems for you. Better to swell into a menacing spiky ball, leaving predators unable to swallow it. Better to think of it as a red lentil in a pea shooter. Better to go slow or it will pop too soon. Better to remember that while it may be fine in your mouth, it will stick to your face. Better use a 12' × 12' tarp. Better to roll it on a steel table, called a marver, into an even cylinder. Better to work with wet roots. Better to press one nostril tight shut. Better to check behind you. Better to have it go *shiko-shiko* in the mouth. Better to attach a nozzle. Better to heat the part we want to move, flash the part we want to keep warm. Better to think of it as a bundle of corks tied together with string. Better practise in your driveway with a paper cup. It's better to keep it in the glory hole, as hot as you can handle, just to the point when you lose control, count to five, then bring it back to the bench and start shaping the glass.

MEMO

re: ligion

see below
regarding
the above

GEST

This is the book of the generations of Adam.   Winded by the squeeze after twelve hours,
In the day that God created man,   five minutes apart. Duck conversation, grip the table leg.
in the likeness of God made he him;   Freeze in the driveway. The jolting car is a relentless
male and female created he them; and blessed   midway ride you regret instantly. Why do
them, and called their name   those people arrange grocery bags in trunks? Why are they
Adam, in the day when they were   jogging? Why aren't they crouched over the pavement
created. And Adam lived   felled by the fierce shock of flesh clamping in on itself for
an hundred and thirty years, and begat   the longest minute every four minutes. After four
a son in his own likeness, after his image;   more hours, they hit three minutes apart.
and called his name   Cling to my neighbour's words: 'I wouldn't exactly call it pain.' But
Seth: and the days of Adam after   I would, I would exactly call it pain more exactly than
he had begotten Seth were eight hundred years: I've ever called anything pain before. Gut
and he begat sons and daughters: and all the days   packed with tacks, demonic blood
that Adam lived were nine hundred and   pressure cuff around the belly, an imploding
thirty years: and he died. And Seth lived an   star, the instant vitrification of organs, a
hundred and five years, and begat Enos: and   cinderblock forced up the yin yang, a
Seth lived after he begat Enos eight hundred   thousand salmonella cramps in concert,
and seven years, and begat sons and daughters: and   reverse time-lapse peony unblooming
all the days of Seth were nine hundred and twelve   into a hot pink fist, a truck full of
years; and he died. And Enos lived ninety   rocks wheeling onto me, pausing a minute on
years, and begat   the bump. Treading water, then seized, treading, seized, the swimming
Cainan: and Enos lived after   girl in *Jaws* rewound, played a hundred times over. After
he begat Cainan eight hundred and fifteen   three hours, two minutes apart, each contraction
years, and begat sons and daughters: ninety seconds long. Nobody told. Who ever said
and all the days of Enos were nine hundred and   a second hand 'sweeps.' The fine red
five years: and he died. And Cainan lived seventy years, and   blade on the school clock
begat Mahalaleel: and Cainan lived after he begat Mahalaleel eight hundred and forty years,
and begat sons and daughters: and all the days of Cainan were nine hundred and ten years:
and he   snags on every fraction of the minute. With every fourth-half pie my life   died.
And Mahalaleel lived sixty and five years, and begat Jared: and Mahalaleel   lifts. Billions
lived after he begat Jared eight hundred and thirty years,   of women have done this how.
and begat sons and daughters: and all the days   Done it more than once how. Pain inspires
of Mahalaleel were eight hundred ninety and five   unholy bestial noises but my animal
years: and he died. And Jared   is a cat, in the still dark under the porch steps. My mum
lived an hundred sixty and two years, and he begat Enoch: and Jared lived   birthed me,
after he begat Enoch eight hundred years, and   her mum birthed her and I birth you and

begat sons and daughters: and all the days of Jared   you will birth your daughter who
were nine hundred sixty and two years: and   will birth her daughter: together we are like
he died. And Enoch lived sixty and five years, and begat   those nesting Russian dolls you
Methuselah: and Enoch walked with God after he   crack open in the middle. Even today
begat Methuselah three hundred years, and begat   half a million women die in childbirth,
sons and daughters: and all the days of Enoch were   one a minute. In Sub-Saharan Africa
three hundred sixty and five years: and Enoch   a woman has a one in twenty chance of
walked with God: and he *was* not; for God took   dying. The cardiotocograph needles
him. And Methuselah lived an hundred eighty and   trace your heart and my contractions
seven years, and begat Lamech: and Methuselah lived after   in tandem, the sawtooth-
he begat Lamech seven hundred eighty and two years, and begat   scribbled paper
sons and daughters: and all the days of Methuselah   coming and coming, hour after hour,
were nine hundred sixty and nine years: and he died.   falling in tidy folds into a deep
And Lamech lived an hundred eighty and   open drawer. Billions of women. Feet planted
two years, and begat a son: and he   in soft dirt or on hieroglyphed birthing bricks or
called his name Noah, saying,   strapped into metal stirrups or held by midwife, sister,
This *same* shall   partner, mother. Push for as long as it takes the ant to climb over my
comfort us concerning our   toes and for six nods of the branch in the breeze and for
work and toil of our   six counts from the nurse. Push for one two three four five six
hands,   because   of   the   one   Come   on   now   nice   hard
ground which the LORD hath cursed. And   Lamech   push for three   four   five
lived after he begat Noah five six Thatta girl you can do this you can tear yourself a
hundred   ninety   and   five   new   one   you   can   snap   yourself   in
years,   and   begat   half,   so   this   is   what   they   mean   by 'torn limb   from
sons   and   daughters: and all   the   days   of   limb,' you can push a   haystack   through a
Lamech   were   seven   hundred   needle   you   can   force   your   insides   outside
seventy   and   seven   four   five   six   one   two   three   with   a   big
years: and   he   breath   we   can   see   her   coming   and   three   four
died.   And   Noah   with   one   more   breath
was   five   hundred   years   who   is   coming,   who   is
old: and   Noah   begat   Shem,   Ham,   my   insides   and
Japheth.   you   emerge   and   for   you   I   would   do
This   is   the   book   *this*
of   the   generations
fourteen   billion   times   over.

COULD YOU LIFT A PIANO OFF A CHILD?

Do you know what
pertussis is? Is
there a live chainsaw
lodged in the log
you're sleeping like?
Are you someone's very
personal pizza? You
blank, having
answered a thousand
questions since naptime
with a) interesting, I'm
not sure or b) bullshit
based on your sketchy
recall of the water cycle.
Is your life a ceaseless
thesis defence? How
do cows jump over
moos? Orange
who? Where
is the barrel for these
monkeys? Did you
water the lush chia
Shrek head? Do
you seriously think that
piano will collapse, perhaps
under a steady drip of
cartoon Steinways?
Would you rather b) sink
the credit line or
a) have a super sour
gummy horn growing

out of your cheek? I trip
over your heart; does
it b) jangle or c)
squeak? Why is it so
loud now and roving,
always underfoot?
Is Shrek not bald?
You explain that ants
can reach the size
of trombones, forgetting
the book is in French.

WITHOUT YOU

I wander lonely as a clod
in a bondless ble sky.
I'm living in a bbble,
the little engine
that cold.

I miss being a nit.

Me and my big
moth, devoring
every planet y'all
were in. Only
Mars and Earth
can sstain life now.
What a clsterfck!

I've lost ten ponds.
I've been hiding in the
hose reading *The History
of Tom Jones, a Fondling*.
I need my fond pot back.

I am ardor's American
neighbor. At the la,
grass skirts hla;
I slmp in a
mm.

I'm in the Salt.

I know I was sed
bt I miss that sing.

I THOUGHT YOU WERE DIFFERENT

Like begins as a liquid
but closes to a quick stop,
voiceless. A lick
withdrawn. Lake
drained dry.

I didn't say I liked it.
I said I, like, liked it.
I wasn't all like, I liked it.

The Parker Street mansion
wheezed and moulted
but we liked
to show prospective
roommates the third-floor
shared kitchen view,
downtown glistering to the left
and straight ahead the dark heaps
of Grouse Mountain, furring
into night, and one, who informed
us her regimen included two
hours of grooming and who
dickered about price, just
glanced at the window
and said, I don't like
views.

I don't like vistas.
Hold the pie.
Don't care to look a deer in the eye.
I don't like the nightlife or to boogie or piña coladas.
I don't like that.

Like many Canadians, I am
like a bird on a wire. Like
many Americans I am like
a rhinestone cowboy. Like
many dual citizens I'm like
a two-timing, fence-sitting,
fusion-cuisine-eating flip-
flopper, entertaining two
unlike ideas at once
according to the fellow in
that rock crystal hat I like.

Please take a moment
to Like my page. Like
many Canadians, I am
likeable. Like many citizens of
the world I find the thumbs
up an obscene gesture. Careful
whom you Like.

Earn the respect of native speakers
by using English fillers such as *uh*,
like and *um*. You will likely
come across as more authentic
and, like, earn the respect of *um*.

And metaphor was all like,
you reflect similarities but
I actually, like, create them
and I was all like, you just
bash stuff together and don't
come clean about it and
metaphor was like, if you hate
metaphor so much why did you

just use one and I was like,
you're a pain in the ass and
metaphor was like, Ah! and
I said the *like* was implied there
and metaphor was like, why
do you have to be so
explicit it's like explaining
jokes and I was like
Ah! Really? Is it *like* that? and
metaphor was all like
Touché and we crossed
imaginary swords.

Do you adore red,
red you can't liken
to any love? Do you
admire the silk-like
lining of her trench
coat, row upon row
of items that could be
paired for curve, give,
the way the feathers
fall? Do you like
comparison
shopping?

Things are not really
the same. It's always
just as if
they were the same.
It's in the almost
that we ride. Why
everything's moving
all the time, like.

CALCULOGUE

BILL: hELLO, LIZ.
LIZ: hI.
BILL: Shh, LIZ. SEE LOIS?
LIZ: Eh?
BILL: LOIS. ShE'S LEZ.
LIZ: Eh?
BILL: ShE'S SLOBBISh. ShE BOOZES. ShE'S LEZ.
LIZ: Oh.
BILL: SEE ShE?
LIZ: hOLLIE?
BILL: LEZBO.
LIZ: Oh.
BILL: ShE OOZES LEZBO. ShE BOSSES. ShE LOBBIES. ShE'S BOLShIE. ShOE SIZE II. SEE LESLIE?
LIZ: LEZBO?
BILL: BI. SEE ShELLIE?
LIZ: ShELLIE'S LEZBO?
BILL: Oh, ShELLIE'S LEZBO.
LIZ: ShELLIE?
BILL: Shh, ShIZZLE. ShE SELLS ShELL OIL, LOOB. ShE LOSES hOSES. ShE LOBS BIBLES.
LIZ: hELL'S BELLS, ShELLIE'S LEZ. ShE SOLO?
BILL: Eh?
LIZ: ShELLIE SIZZLES. ShE BOILS. ShE'S ShOBIZ! I SLOSh.
BILL: Eh?!
LIZ: I IS LEZ, BOZO. SO Shh. SEE LIZ? LIZ IS SO, SO LEZ.

MEMO

re: gret

I'm over it
and over it

DISPOSABLE THUMBS

I

To My Vermiform Appendix

They took you without
asking. Surgery for
something else, doc
eagerly thrashing behind
the drywall, 'while we're
in there ... ' Just because
you do nothing or
because of something
you might do. If only
they'd cut off my
elbow, I wouldn't have
broken it. Ackee and rhubarb
salad on the menu, that prime
minister still in office, yet
they deemed *you* too shifty-
eyed to keep around. Maybe I
liked you, maybe I didn't
consider you a fifth wheel,
a bomb ticking, worm
turning. Take a kidney out
and at least do some good.
Why do we revile some
vermiform things while others
remain cock of the walk?

I never got to see you, possibly
the longest or lumpiest or
most all-around gorgeous

vermiform appendix on record. Hell,
I don't even know if you
were fixed retrocecally
or not. You may have been
vestigial but you still
stockpiled my gut flora.
What if I run out of gut flora?
What if I need an efferent urinary conduit?
You'd be awesome at that.
Under McBurney's point, three
inches southwest of my
scarred umbilicus,
you don't lie.

11
0 Entries. Try Polenta.

Out of the oven
with the bun yet
it didn't occur to me
to eat either of them

> not an afterthought but
> not a twin either

Does the placenta have a placenta?

> So I was so totally not
> going to eat it but
> it prevents PPD
> so I'm going why not

> Freaked
> about delivering

> the Latin word for cake

If only the permanent organs
worked as hard as the temps

my placenta or yours

> For a festive look, stuff vol-au-vent shells
> my husband carefully removed the membranes

> A strawberry smoothie helps
> you not know which red

plated with crumpled gauze
on the stainless-steel hospital cart

It fed her and could
now feed me, really
having my cake and

As with any uncontrolled meat

but: cannibalism? also
I don't like kale?

III
Tonsillitis

Sit still.
Lots o' sittin'.

No tillin' soil.
No toilin' in silt.
No solo tootin', loon noosin', lino lotionin', loin oilin'.
No onion slittin', sis tossin', snot tinnin', lotto slottin', lint tintin'.
No losin' tools in snits, no tiltin' on listin' stilts, no instillin'
    notions in tots.
No lootin'.
No lit nits.

Loll in silo.
Lilt.
Insist on lions.

VOW

to be your whetted knife
the loofah of your life

door floor's sleeve of rice
nice piece of royal pain

butter-soaked artichoke
cuckoo humming in your clock

free setback variance permit
flannel-nested Netflix hermit

secure line you talk on
hot coals you walk on

invasive yet appealing sumac
our feral kids could make tea from

as koi to your touch screen
dock spider to the dock

as Slinky to the stairs: all quake and
lurch and game to start from the top

Forg~~ive~~me

they were ~~delicious~~

so ~~sweet~~

~~and~~ so ~~cold~~

WHAT IS PROSE

Prose has wit,
war, hot spies,
pirate shows.
It has powers:
a swisher top,
wiser pathos,
towers, a ship,
parishes. Two
IHOPS. Waters
whose traps I
sap, so whiter
whites. Spa or
showier taps
spew hot airs,
'Poet wash, sir?'
Posh waiters
tow Sharpies,
shower pitas,
pestos awhir,
pastries, how!

How it spears
trophies, was
tops, was heir
to Sears. 'Whip
Thor, asswipe!
Swap heros!' it
whispers to a
hipster. Aw. So
worship a set.

EVEN THE IMPERTURBABLE SPOCK TREMBLES ON THE EDGE OF A PLEASED REACTION.

In the awkward
silence of outer space,
crickets chirr
on the Enterprise
bridge, whose ambient
sounds of a late March
wetland celebrate
you, Spock, glossiest
blackbird, entering through the
swish wicket. You share
indigo-black lacquered hair
with Veronica Lodge and
as with her, we find your human
moments a little obscene,
confetti-cannoning spores.
The blessing of the Kohanim
couched in your Vulcan
salute, almost more love
than we can take.
My brother was allowed
to watch because he came
from Mars, but the babysitter
hugged me to illustrated
bible stories, fed me pink
wintergreen pucks until
my mouth was a clean toilet.
Kirk has his combative face on, whirls,
half whirls, whirls back around,
orbiting the binary blue stars

of your polyester jersey
and eyeshadow, more fetching
than any in the universe, more
lovely than the name DeForest,
who spits and blusters and
inspires only a slight lift in
your eyebrows at finding spring
peepers under your console.
Your sparkling re- and de-
materializations fizz the best.
In life you drove home
to an icy Alberta town
of fewer than two thousand
life forms and no Tim Hortons.
In life you advocated equal pay
for Nichelle Nichols because
it was only logical. Your hair
was matte, your features
filed down. You wrote poems.
You were a genial, plaid-
sportcoat-wearing uncle
gamely narrating the pseudo-
science of *In Search Of...* who
understood that erotic life dwells
in another, sleeker
dimension, a
prolonged
sparkling
transport.

BEE HOLE

it's what you bee out of
as opposed to A hole
where the bees was
none of your
bees is
be

hold
the leaf-
ing maple
the bees left
air in a   all shape
  ees had   een vehemently
holed up there queen deep
in the   all of   ees

BEE HOLE

B-side view: spit-roasted
boar's mouth apple
having rolled out
impossibility
of there
in

the
mind
of someone
here the gallery
shark sunk into the
plastic belly of the bear

BEE BALL

                         here
                     if you had
                 been here hon if only
              you hadn't been there you would
           have seen it a whole ball of scribbled
         babble would do a fat lot of good showing you
      what was wholly here and in the middle you would
         not have seen the   even then but all
             the biz around her pointed to her being in
                there no talk only workers their avid
                   sparking twine apprising you if
                       you could only be here
                          hon I guess you
                            had to be
                             there

TRANSIT

Shambling through sand in Patagonia
and Columbia wear, we queue up
for a rare wow. The Sky

News guy twiddles the azimuth,
lures with the roulette of glimpsing
a Venusian ring of light or black drop

for which we'll each steal a few extra
seconds by playing dumb at the eyepiece
then circle back to the end of the line again.

We watch the shot sun without looking at it,
just as we can watch without looking at our
backlit children hunched, picking over the shore.

Call and call them to a turn at the scope
but they hunker at the lake's wet lip, mylar
glasses flung, because they'll catch it

next century, something like water already
trickling quickly from the pebbles and
shells in their hands.

SEA CLIFF PARK

I put lots of really nice and smart people
who are religious in my pipe and smoke it.
We wave at each other across the municipal
splash pad. I'm pretty sure they put their pants on
both legs at a time. The giant tomato smiles
down and empties itself over ecstatic shrilling.
When pregnant and under the influence of
my new greatest fear, I spontaneously develop
taboos: Do not wear red-flowered underwear.
Do not throw away photographs of babies. Babies
I know but also the strange babies tucked in new
picture frames, deckle-edged junk-flyer babies.
I know how foreshadowing works.
Someday my daughter will sort through
my books and all the little children will fall out.

My Life is supposed to be good for you.
My Death comes layered in a tall parfait
glass. My Trust is available in smooth
or studded. My Wisdom tastes best sucked through
a strainer straw. My Luck includes ends and
pieces which can't be sold to the fancy-
packed market. My Goodness contains gluten
and alcohol which may not dissipate
when baked. My Loyalty smells better the
longer you have it on. My Peace projects
an open, bombastic, high-amplitude
sound. My Pride is Roundup Ready. My Joy,
featuring gob-side access, raises and
lowers the ranging arms and lumpbreaker

and rotates the cowls. My Hart interrupts
the flea life cycle. My Wit has a horse-
blanket quality. There's no need to soak
my Beauty. My entire Confidence
creaks and wobbles, especially at high
speeds. In March 2011,
the Coca-Cola company purchased
my Honesty. My Zest for men will not
leave a sticky film on you. My goji,
avocado and quince Faith foams in a
canvas gift pouch. My Courage is proud to
be a Glock-stocking dealer. The size of
my Hope is measured from the middle hole.
My Hope breathes menthol cool. It comes from the

Philippines. Friendly representatives
of my Hope would love to consider your
giving options over the phone now. My
Honour vibrates at three different speeds.
My Compassion usually arrives
in five to thirteen business days. In six
to seven weeks my Humility will
ship. My Sincerity pops with lavish
hand beading. My Respect is limited
to the continental U.S. Image-
conscious women who can also enjoy
a cocktail are my Devotion's target
audience. My Liberty will tow me
on a flatbed. My Luvs leak through the night.

Reading that old ode, apple
blossoms waxing the window, the hour
pools, pipes and timbrels
rumple, lift, forget
an appointment, that there are
appointments. Oh,
the learning outcomes!
By the end of this poem,
readers will be able to
formulate and *implement*
acceptable interpretive modalities.
Readers will be able to
<action verb>. Readers will be able
to *sandblast*. Readers will be able to
guzzle, flay and *kablooey*
in a measurable manner. Using
only staples from Staples, append
an exit survey to monitor efficacy.
Why did you choose to read
this poem? Did the poem help you
meet those investment objectives?
Verbs to avoid: *perceive, enjoy,*
realize, learn, be glazed with rain
water. Was there too much
reading involved? Would you
recommend the poem to
other readers seeking similar
outcomes? Do you now know all
ye need to know? Do you now *feel*
confident that your negative
capability is transferrable to, e.g.,
other pharmaceutical validation protocols?

I

Your PIN is unique to
you know my undying
hip technology along
and under your tongue
ace-to-face transaction
old your legs around m
 education costs.
ow many fingers you c
your four-digit PIN w
oose your four-digit P
that certain zing to the
shield your Private Id
holding it, how soft it
or upon purchase, you
Swipe and sign or chip
so good I can't even te
purchasing goods for
hip and PIN securely
over your hips when I
warp and strip abrasio
hen swiping your strip
                 Swipe
lick and bite.
for your own protection
inside you again, if only
Your unique PIN will pr
in and again and again u
on an annual basis, or su
anytime, day or night, yo

Swipe towards you or in
your every scar and freck
   Insert the chip and
hale the sheets, until you
our magnetic strip out a
ur voice, the grit and oil
strip towards the cashier
please return the bottom
can rub the magnetic str
can you remember the s
number of children unde

34.70

Forgot your PIN? Enter
ember feeling the pang of
PIN? Enter your email ad
t's sweetest sweat. How c
ortization, or a 25-year m
about when I licked your

5.97%

sensitive materials, so be
that way again, I crave th
raudulent activity.

Any woman who's gone to this guy's office
knows he really loves Superman.
– ratemydoctor.com

graphed by Christopher Re
soon after her epidural, was
This vintage Man of Steel is
was evacuated of clots, spo
signed by George Reeves, '
grasped with ring forceps to
some rust and the usual wea
adequate and blood-tinged
This plastic Man of Steel is
female, age 57, presenting
he inside is nearly spotless
hemostatically intact, but th
*Box is also mint.
clamped, cut, and suture lig
the usual age-related wear,
with no adhesions or lesions,
 it's a bird, it's a plane, it's
a portion of the tubal stump
   The 'Holy Grail' of Super
bilateral salpingo-oophorect
buckle comes w/ FREE belt
with Metzenbaum scissors.
. As with any vintage issues
ovarian pedicles isolated by
Great Scott, Lois! What hav
proceeded to the abdomen,
day shipping to the U.S.A. on

with clamps and hot cautery
this Man of Steel, all wood
divided in the midline.
-year-old female presenting
a big beanbag Man of Steel
now catheterized, and drain
ed of about 200 cc of urine
signia, and has a black beze
rectus muscle divided, hum
small rip in the back but no
-transverse uterine incision
and repaired with tape.
and tissue were removed to
lighter could be removed to
     Cannulate the left fallop
. Currently out of stock! Try
the endocervical canal, into
   This cool collectible Man o
visceroperitoneum closed wi
just a small scuff.
piously irrigated. 10mm suct
n of Steel's S-shield logo on
a red rubber catheter was use
the arms move up and down
in the dorsal supine position
in a punching action. It has
abdomen opened in layers w
never been played with!
moderate amount of bleedin
ssic all-wood hands and feet
ncurrent elective sterilization
No. 75, issued 11-17-1992.
C-section for abruption. Pat

cratch visible in my pics.
infant's head delivered and
autographed by Margot Kid
ing single-toothed tenaculu
Krytpo Ray gun. Mail to U
quick delivery of infant and
auctioning naked figure only
was delivered and handed ov
fingers and ten toes! No flaw
nel conducted sponge count.
with glow-in-the-dark hands
unfortunately a name is scra
uccessful. Infant cried spont
name could be buffed out if
because of previous caesaria
figure comes without outfit
Cord blood was obtained fo
lass display case shaped like
living female infant, vertex,
Sorry about the cape.
nasopharynx were suctioned
sharpener is in his chest! Jus
a viable male infant, 7 lbs. 4
   No marks or loose joints!
elivered living infant, female
Folds out to 6 ½' high for st
all 20 issues for this incredib
Apgar scores 9 and 9. After 5
his big beanbag Man of Steel
s closed with 26 metal staples
in any way as an actual gun

III

ttention that certain me
Surfactants we
never harassed or threa
illion litres of oil into t
workplace environment.
history of blowing thin
gest spill in U.S. histor
viously highly confiden
blouse and otherwise o
e oil, deceased mamma
luminum foil and wrap
vidence of misconduct
oil on mammals or bird
nor verbal threats.
We trust you can
cost 11 lives.
mosphere of camaraderi
mage control. Our reput
y to misinterpret friendly
birds and mammals.
The gross over-
ess can be avoided if th
ogether in the workplace
usual mortality events in
age control. The optics
dolphins and other seali
assment. These unfound
her attire. Coworkers ha
grievances seriously, in
lungs and adrenal gland
zon. The impact on bird

limate of mutual respect
dispersants. Minimizing
nimal toxicity to sealife
rust. That trust is very i
in question was not pre
no way inappropriate o
mental losses. Cost rec
to be transferred to anot
economic and ecologica
mutually satisfactory an
that we are dedicated to
rt skirt. Appropriate busi
rts of dead sealife washi
artment. We are dedicati
her department. Undo str
uced to a matter of 'spin'
orkplace environment.

The Disney Princesses outnumber you.

The Disney Princesses grace pencil cases, socks, toothpaste, bandages.

Soon they will appear on dog food and pink insulation. The next time you go to your mechanic he will offer you the Disney Princesses timing belt.

Lesbians worry their daughter will catch flak about hemp overalls and flax sandwiches, so they buy her the Disney Princesses backpack.

But even if you wanted to shield your child from the Disney Princesses, you couldn't. Someone will lend her a Disney Princesses eraser, and she'll be hooked, because the Disney Princesses are like crack or PEZ.

The Disney Princesses bloom in threes, fused at the hips.

The Disney Princesses stick together, at least the white ones do.

The Disney Princesses are Charlie's Angels without the guns.

> *I'm offering for sale a brand new Pink Disney Princess Flip-Open Slumber Sofa. When it is in the sofa shape, it has Cinderella, Snow White and Sleeping Beauty on the front. When you open it to sleep on, the blanket has Cinderella, Snow White and Belle. The entire cover can be unzipped and laundered.*

The Disney Princesses don't wear pants.

Disney Princesses are post-feminist.

I've never seen Jasmine, Mulan and Pocahontas together on snowboots.

Disney Princesses are not ideological.

Disney Princesses love you a lot, as long as you are a girl.

The Disney Princesses' anthem says

> *~there's a place where hope and dreams can last for all time~*

In other words, the Disney Princesses would rather never be satisfied.

Each Disney Princess has a male love interest who never appears on the thermoses or underpants.

The Disney Princesses prefer hanging out on your pillowcase talking about hope and dreams with you.

That way you and the Disney Princesses can love each other and not look suspicious.

The Disney Princesses do not associate with Barbie; they are virtuous maidens from days of yore and Barbie keeps gynecological appointments on her BlackBerry.

The Disney Princesses had oatmeal and quail eggs for breakfast. Barbie had a diet pill and a grape Pop-Tart.

The Disney Princesses titter at Hannah Montana. She became a human woman, and her wall of socks came tumbling down.

Disney Princesses can be unzipped and laundered.

Disney Princesses have a rubber backing.

Disney Princesses may warp in the dishwasher.

Disney Princesses can become unstable and tip forward, causing risk of fall.

Disney Princesses may link together inside the intestines.

Do not inflate the Disney Princesses.

The Disney Princesses are a choking hazard.

MEMO

re: aches

as with all
else we do, the heart
does it more

FOR LAUREN AND ANDREA

1   Find a river.

2   Know the rules. Marriage is regulated by your state or province. You have to buy a marriage licence. Most sporting goods stores sell them.

3   Watch for slow-moving patches of deep, or any area going from deep to shallow or shallow to deep.

4   Bait your hook. If you are using one of the fingers, you need to push the ring through the end of the finger and work the length of the finger on to the ring until the finger gets to the end of the ring, then pull the tip of the ring out through the finger to expose it. Pinch off the remainder of the finger about 1 inch away from the ring so that a small part dangles from the end. If you are using salmon roe or corn kernels, simply push a couple of pieces onto the ring just past the barb.

5   Always propose slightly upstream, to the 11 o'clock position as you face the river. This allows your proposal to drift with the current and appear more lifelike. Most prospective fiancées face upstream and wait for proposals to wash towards them. If you spook the fiancées, you should wait about 20 minutes before attempting to propose again in that spot.

6   Let the proposal drift, tip up and about face level. Once the proposal gets past you, the line will start to tighten up, so keep your eyes on where the line is going in your peripheral vision. Any small tugs could be the proposal bouncing off rocks or it could be love tasting the bait. Wait for love to

take the bait. You will know when you have love by the huge pulling feeling.

7   If you've hooked it, steady yourself so as not to lose the love as it violently thrashes about in the water. Rainbow love is particularly hard to manage, as it's been known to leap and 'tail-walk' when hooked. Once you have the love reeled in to shore, take your net and gently scoop it up.

8   Please keep only what you will eat.

WHY THRASH YOUR OARS

None of the swimmers says, Hey,
why do we not ask where the
beef is anymore? When did we
all start saying bucket list? They
cavort and thump your leaky
boat, whizz over your gunwales.
They used to beg you to get
with the program. You think
of those dreams where
your voice doesn't
come out except
they're the ones
with mouths gushing
ocean. They're not bothered.
Their nostrils evolve up the face
and over into blowholes so fast
it's like watching bowling balls
roll. You say the only thing
more embarrassing than being
really bad at bowling is
being really good at bowling.
Bilge soaks your socks.
Why can't you just sing? Why
can't you accept that at the end
of the day we are going forward?
Just write that bucket list,
even if all it says is
buckets
buckets
buckets

Dunes and back is 8k, Sleepy Hollow and back 9k, Black Willow 15. Every route a straight there-and-back, I learn to gauge when I am half-baked. Top of the foot, left hip, right shoulder, these are the spots where, in a Tylenol commercial, the scarlet burrs flash. Talking about running is as tedious as telling someone your dreams; taking my cue from the Surrealists, I do it anyway. As a girl I heard that runners become addicted to the dolphins. Oxygen in, carbon dioxide out. Coal in, sulphur dioxide out. Uranium in, radioactivity out. Fukushima's in, Chernobyl's out. The only other time I could have so blithely shed a toenail was in childbirth. My shadow drags me by the ankles along the asphalt road, and in that darker faster body, pale pebbles and twigs appear to rain down inexorably, a diagram of digestion, a snow globe. Today there is a 20k charity run, and although I am neither running 20k nor wearing an orange race bib – orange could mean leukemia, ms, the ndp, motorcycle safety or feral cats – spectators assume I'm participating and shout *You're half-way there! Courage, sister!* and I, too tired to pant out a confession, just raise my fist *Woo!* Point Pelee is biodiversity's tall tale: cattails and lopseed to scalloped sand to swamp bush swallowtails to Northern forest hugger-mugger to beach scree, cactus mats, red cedar savannah, vine-hung Carolinian – I can imagine I've run a long way. Running was supposed to help me tap my own steam, but I begin to suspect I am in thrall to something. Kilometres to the tip: 10. Kilometres to the Fermi Nuclear Plant: 61.4. Kilometres to the Davis-Besse Nuclear Plant: 61.5. Kilometres to the liquor store: 6.9. Thanks to an athletic brother, I trained the next lane over from Victor Davis, learned my strokes from an Olympian named 'El Profe,' spent hours before and after school in the pool. Never won a race, not even on Track and Field day, when the kids who ate Lucky Charms and watched *Hogan's Heroes* after school left me in their dust. One leg slightly shorter than the other, I run iambically. Weaker than a newborn possum, weaker even than the entire tablespoon of possums lifting en masse. At eight years old I filled out Charles Atlas's comic-book ad for ❑ bulkier arms ❑ broader chest and back ❑ tireless legs ❑ magnetic personality. I was tired of being HALF A MAN! My father, marking calculus exams at the kitchen table and probably needing a laugh, was asked for a stamp. Legs go on without me: a heartbeat, a dog, a two-stroke engine. Running from, running to. Dogged or dogged. To get the outside inside. To make heat. To the sandspit at the tip, to be the southernmost woman in Canada. You could win this valuable trophy. From grading essays. From the beginning of time and the eighteenth century, croquettes had a lot of skills in wits yet kept their chatty intact. From an ache without a reason. For all they know, I'm a world-class sprinter recovering from an injury. After a wind storm, the forest a gym full of trust exercises. Every day I walk up and hoist my pass for the kiosk ranger and then start running, into the park and back, and after a while she knows me and I don't even have to show my pass, but I do, because I don't just run into the woods without permission, and weeks go by: her daily smile and wave, a grin through the glass, a two-handed flap, a curled-finger air caress, an intimate nod, *There goes the runner*, she thinks, wowed by my athleticism and high-tech shoes, by that formidable woman who's old enough to be her mother but can run for a solid hour or more and look at those ripped calves! One day as I'm approaching the end, slowing, hot-cheeked and radiating triumph, the ranger putters outside her kiosk, she's fiddling with a green sign, classic fan ruse, and I turn down my iPod and she calls out, in a voice reserved for toddlers, *Have a nice walk?* It's supposed to be two steps each for inhale and exhale, like *Hey Hey, Ho Ho!* (you can choose what's got to go!) but swimmers' lungs swallow up six beats, as in *Hey Hey Hey* and *Ho Ho Ho*, as in Fat Albert and Santa Claus, both of whom would beat me in a race. The trunk rises to bronchi, to bronchioles, to clusters of alveoli, which drop to the road with a sigh. Huff and puff. Pufnstuf. Hufflepuff. For all they know, I am a slo-mo Englishman on the beach in *Chariots of Fire*. In 1790 the Caldwell First Nation ceded Point Pelee to the government in a treaty they didn't sign. FirstEnergy Corp. fell to $43.76 at the close in New York after a report that engineers discovered a thirty-foot hairline crack in the concrete shell of its Davis-Besse nuclear plant. The green sign says THE STABLE FLIES ARE BITING. Buffeting sounds too soft for what the lake wind is doing. The run-on sentence takes no breaks. In the 1950s thousands of people sardined onto the beaches in polka-dot bikinis and jolly clouds of DDT. With the hot dog and beer stands gone, the beach is bare now, on the horizon twin plumes from the Fermi dragon's northward snout. Heffalump. Hasselhoff. Puffin fluff. Whiffenpoof. Among the Canada geese, a white swan. We really love Swarovski's luminous and modern statement piece that celebrates the wonder of nature, that it's one-ply and breaks down easily in today's low-flow toilet systems. We love that it's soft and solid. In thrall to oxygen. The green sign says ACTUALLY YOU ARE OLDER THAN MY MOTHER. The sky becoming less Sky Blue. It's Cobalt but I say who would pay $6.40 admission to a National park just to rape a jogger. There's one road, same in and out, no getaways, who would pay, thank the kiosk ranger for the owling map, park the car Jazz Blue by the side of the road which you're not supposed to do anyway and French Navy

Blue there are wardens patrolling for that, drag a jogger Denim Blue into the woods, risk being seen leaving Ultramarine by the same attendant, and if he can see Ink my reflective piping surely he'll know Midnight I can take him Black Blue at the bottom of a well. Running for president. Running for Dummies. Running out of oil. Are we running out of oil and gas? Are we running out of IP addresses? Time is running out for Greece. Popeye's ran out of chicken yesterday in Rochester, N.Y. following a special on chicken. Running for the cure. Exactly what happens if we run out of water? It's running in the background of your iPhone. The passing cars wag their windshield wipers at me but I laugh at the sleet in my moisture-wick technology. A late starter and lifelong weakling, I have no varsity records to haunt me. A rush from behind and then the great yellow claws before my eyes, only just curling up from an octave-wide span the raptor prepared before, finding the weird neon rabbit too large to pluck, she thought better of it. Morning and evening, trunk shadows spring across the road, hair standing on end, tamed only briefly at noon by the licked palm of the sun. Scan the hoof-pocked shoulder for things I've lost: park pass, glove, 1–2 percent of muscle mass every year after forty. Running on solar energy. Just leave the car running. Other locations ran out of chicken too, the $4.99 special too good to pass up. Running on fumes. Running on JavaScript. California at Risk of Running Out of Money by March. Windsor–Detroit Running Out of People. Running out of breath. Running out of bandwidth. Are we running out of stuff? You left the water running. We just kinda ran out of gas. Squirrels rush around, carbo loading. I consider walking and the turkey vultures on the bare silver branch turn, adjust their footing, one lifts a dusty sail. Dummies for President. You left the money running. Oil and gas running out of grease. Before I lace up my Just Do Its I pull on my Designed for Sport, Crafted for Life and if it's cold my Refuse to Compromise with Because We Take Your Running as Seriously as Our Own and, to keep my head warm, Let's Make Excellent Happen and Don't Just Go With It, Run With It and under all that, if you must know, I'm Bringing the Legacy into the Present and America's First Name in Comfort Since 1901. Winter-bleached marsh reeds still two metres high all around, we traverse the boardwalk, fleas on a golden dog. Popeye running out of breath. Olive Oyl running out of gas. The North wind sculpts the Davis-Besse plume into a rearing caterpillar. At this rate I could circle the Earth in 208.7 days. Let me just charge my iPod. Laid end to end, you could circle the Earth with: the nerves in your body; a day's worth of oil consumption, in fifty-five-gallon steel drums; a year's worth of discarded ink cartridges; a day's worth of plastic water bottles dropped in U.S. landfills; one quarter of all Barbie dolls manufactured; one fifth of the eggs produced in North Carolina in 1980; 2.2 million human small intestines. It's amazing there's anywhere to step. Breath too good to pass up. Fumes for breath. Breath for bandwidth. It's breathing in the background of your iPhone. Davis-Besse was shuttered for more than three months in 2010 after workers discovered coolant leaking through cracks in some reactor-head nozzles. A scrap of mink coat scuttles across the boardwalk. No choice but to run south, I can't reassure the doe – who glances back over her shoulder, trots ahead, glances back – that I'm not tracking her, can't avoid staring at the sun, the scene before me perforated with afterimages, an evershifting spray of blue-green bullet holes. Would you rather be an elite marathoner, vomit and pee in the street, never breaking pace, or the slower participant who can relax, wave to the fans, step in it? $4.99 for the cure. $4.99 for spinach. We just kinda ran out of ip addresses. ip for Popeye. Leaks and reactor corrosion prompted FirstEnergy to close the plant from 2002 to 2004, while the company retrained or replaced workers who ignored signs of damage. I know the lake froze overnight because legs hoisted the floating ducks. I am a cheetah and a bullet-train and I kick sand in faces! Leaves flake off, revealing a mess of nests, spots on a lung. Two steps forward, one sore back. I'll trade that raccoon my breathable mesh and responsive midsole for the ability to see with my hands. Litter depresses except for the mint Aero foil, evergreen. Flying squirrels don't, really, but naming goes a long long way from canopy to forest floor. One nail would puncture a lung but you rest on a thousand points unharmed, because of the word *bed*. Think up, think the roaring sun, think the inch taller, think daybreak swelling fog, think a dew-balloon glissading down a pine needle, hitting the gold back of a frog who jumpcuts into light in Lycra shorts, think bed, think that sitting up in the dark and feeling for your socks and glasses is another kind of going to bed. Over the last decade, one resident ran out of Detroit every twenty-two minutes. Oil for president. Just leave Windsor–Detroit running. What happens if we run out of background? I never squandered the lucid dreams of my childhood, placing myself on my mark for the Running Long Jump and in midleap flying just a touch, enough to win but not enough to arouse suspicion. The only monster on the predawn road is me, unable to avoid the snails popping underfoot. I am the worst nuisance on the beach! January's paraffin lake, grey in the guttering sun. In the marsh a Great Northern Loon or Red-Breasted Merganser or jagged log or Doc Marten boot or boot with foot severed at the ankle flaring into a squawk and flight at the skipped stones of collateral earbud music. Oil left the water running. Are we running out of solar? We just kinda chickened out. Do I stop at organ donation or give them all of me so they can section me into inch-thick slabs, organize me into drawers, invite medical students to gaze and gently prod and the ones who got into it for the money will be the worst lovers. Do not judge a person's politics by their running playlist and anyway when Pitbull said, 'I like that dale mama,' I thought he was saying, 'I like that Dalai Lama.' Kick the black ribbon of road behind me, then turn around and pull it back into place before the warden comes by. I've held up the 99 percent perspiration end of the deal. Do I give a shit if the hot peppers drop off my ratemyprofessors.com page? Running time: 1 hr 26 min. Rated PG for scenes of peril and fantasy violence, brief crude humour, intense themes, mild language, depiction of a smoking caterpillar. But why ask the Dalai Lama to 'bend it on over'? At twenty I wore roomy hippie smocks to protect myself from the panopticonic cultural surveillance of female bodies. Now I deflect the gaze with my skin-tight polypropylene leggings. It helps that nobody's looking now. Leaf pile: recto yellow, verso buff. Recto scarlet, verso plain brown wrapper. My feet strike the road and later the road strikes back, but in the delirious middle they high-five for a while. In thrall to the dolphins. I expend enough energy to power a head-mounted 100-watt lightbox sign that says COKE. Drawing a tree, we forget the half living underground, the woman who runs upside-down below me, rooting through packed earth. In 1922 the RCMP destroyed the root cellars of remaining Caldwell First Nation families to ensure they wouldn't return. The damaged structure poses no safety hazard to Davis-Besse, located twenty-one miles southeast of Toledo, said Jennifer Young, a First-Energy spokeswoman. Rooted in, rooted out. Low on water, the return trip is an Escher staircase. Poems either go too far or not far enough. Further warmer than farther. Farther further than father. Feathers fatter than either. The lake thaws, yanks their legs back under. Energy corporations always hire female spokespersons. I feel all apple pie about the tar sands. The ATV riders think I am crazy and I think they are crazy, each of us considering ourselves the one actually doing something. You move to the country for the stillness and peace or you move to the country so you can raise hell. You are neighbours. We believe the crack issues could be resolved relatively quickly, said Michael Worms, an analyst at BMO Capital Markets in New York. In thrall to it all. And kilometres to go before I sleep and hope to wake up manic enough.

GOOD GUYS

Good guys do not bomb your buzz with an encyclopedic knowledge of ordnances. Good guys are peace buffs. They say *Little Girls for Mayor.* Sift pink dust into the Sistine stove. Good guys see eye to eye with man-haters, who hate guys. Man-haters are good guys: they may flip bad guys the bird but they do not shoot them in the face for going to school; they are too busy helping women through PTSD in their under-funded offices. If you knew what they know you'd be a man-hater along with the good guys. If abuse always produced abuse, we'd fear the fang-glitter of little girls. I remind the man-hater I love that there are good guys. Good guys include but are not limited to: Stephen Lewis. She will also accept: Marshall, Uncle Herb, Louis, one of the Ramones. Sometimes Tom. Good guys know it's up to them to convert the bad guys. Good guys escort bad guys to their cars, so women can stalk black air, breathe stars. Beware bad guys in the guise of good guys. Good girls does not have the same ring to it. Good girls hurls bad girls over the wall, then hands the good girls a hawk and a tuckpoint trowel. Good girls are the little guy. Good guys say girls will be girls. Good guys sit somewhere on this stuffy bus, peeling a clementine. Good guys let slip the dog's water dish. Good guys get that we call them visionaries for saying things a million little girls folding Kleenex beds for crickets could have told us.

8 ATE ∞

Pleased your phone
number gives you
a row of Os?

All electives being equal,
enrol in the rolling
hummocks of Geology 383.

Seven to some means
several, whatever. Six
or seven are both a few

too many cats. Who
can remember if
we've turned thirty-seven,

maybe forty-nine already.
But she who still counts
her age on fingers

curls them to individual
numbers as to singular
monkey bars. For a year

she stands at the prow
of seven, lead sharpened
by the Swiss Army, shark fin,

bared tooth, even as hers
hail down. She
narrows in on eight. Nine's

just six slung up
to the top bunk
but eight ≥ infinite

yes. Headless
snowmen got no worries
about nothing. She

will lick the split
Oreo of eight, in no
rush but ticking,

an open pocket-
watch from back
in the day.

MEMO

re: verse

here line
the end

LATENCY PERIOD

dormant I collect
pledges for the Swim-
a-thon tongue red
nonpareils off licorice
pipes take oxygen
in through skin
reread L. M.
Montgomery under
leaf litter worry
the tuning wheel of my
Radio Shack radio
smooth as a quarter troll
for Gordon Lightfoot
my pulse a blip
once every several
minutes in the mud-
caked season between
parentlove and peerlust
yearning for yearning
for his voice suspended
between torpor and
passion a song heard
underwater down
there with me and
a large ship
and a gone feelin'

I

yay

vowel hoisted
on sticks
frosty morning
fifth attempt

hah

5 minutes later

II
spire

STOKED
tOKE
Ok
O
On
One
tOne
stOned

III
blurred

WHAT POETRY ISN'T

(a no-tone poem)

Snow. Art. Pity. The
Twitter syphon. A
water hypnotist,
towny therapist
to wintery paths
that irony swept.

Not thy wiretaps,
nor thy pit sweat,
thy twat- or penis-
party. Ew. Not this
nor that. Tipsy, we
thaw tiny tropes:

Not stripey wheat.
Not thy straw pie.
It's not hay, twerp!

Worthy pet, it's an
entropy swath. It
ain't pretty. Who's
Stein to pry what
paint throws. Yet
Pointy Star, whet!
Sharpen to witty
pyrite whatnots.
It's pay — worth ten,
phat twenty, or is
it

NOTES ON THE POEMS

'What is Poetry,' 'What is Prose' and 'What Poetry Isn't' are composed of anagrams of their titles.

'My Fellow Contranym' is built around homonyms that yoke opposite meanings.

There is not even one dirty line in 'Better Blowing.' That's all you.

'Without You''s without u.

'Calculogue' was composed on a Canon LS-863TG handheld calculator.

'Tonsillitis' reduced me to using only letters found in *tonsillitis.*

The following is a variant of 'blurred' in 'Poems for Andy Goldsworthy':

> red
> drop
> in blue
> gut in red
> tuft in
> blue egg
> in red belly
> in blue
> sky in
> ready

You'll find found material in this book from various sources, among them William Carlos Williams, placentophagy message boards, a trout-fishing website, the Bible and Pitbull.

ACKNOWLEDGEMENTS

Thanks to Nicole Markotić for lovingly ruthless editing of this book and for over twenty years of ruthlessly loving poetry together. Thanks also to the brilliant people at Coach House, especially Alana Wilcox, who fine-tuned and made this book. Many others offered advice, edits, complaints and encouragements for the poems in *Throaty Wipes*: Jeramy Dodds, Louis Cabri, Simina Banu, Anne Fleming, Damian Rogers, Tom Dilworth, Heidi Jacobs, Suzette Mayr, Sam Whittaker, Amilcar Nogueira and my supportive family (special thanks to Alex for attentive readings and Geof for 'a twelve-tone poem'). Daily gratitude to my partner, Lori Kennedy, and my small editor Elise Holbrook (who informed me that you can make the word 'onion' with the letters in 'tonsillitis'). A Humanities Research Group Fellowship at the University of Windsor in 2012 afforded me a semester to focus on writing poetry.

Poems in this book first appeared in the following publications: Hazlitt, *The Walrus*, *Touch the Donkey*, *Rampike*, *Matrix*, *This*, *Open Letter*, PRISM, TCR, *Journal of Medical Humanities*, *filling station*, *Canada and Beyond: Journal of Canadian Literature and Cultural Studies* and *50+ Poems for Gordon Lightfoot*.

Susan Holbrook's poetry books are the Trillium-nominated *Joy Is So Exhausting* (Coach House, 2009), *Good Egg Bad Seed* (Nomados, 2004) and *misled* (Red Deer, 1999), which was shortlisted for the Pat Lowther Memorial Award and the Stephan G. Stephansson Award. She lives in Leamington, Ontario, and teaches North American literatures and Creative Writing at the University of Windsor. She is the author of a poetry textbook, *Reading (and Writing About) Poetry* (Broadview Press, 2015) and co-editor, with Thomas Dilworth, of *The Letters of Gertrude Stein and Virgil Thomson: Composition as Conversation* (Oxford, 2010).

Typeset in Albertan.

Albertan was designed by the late Jim Rimmer of New Westminster, B.C., in 1982. He drew and cut the type in metal at the 16pt size in roman only; it was intended for use only at his Pie Tree Press. He drew the italic in 1985, designing it with a narrow fit and a very slight incline, and created a digital version. The family was completed in 2005, when Rimmer redrew the bold weight and called it Albertan Black. The letterforms of this type family have an old-style character, with Rimmer's own calligraphic hand in evidence, especially in the italic.

Printed at the old Coach House on bpNichol Lane in Toronto, Ontario, on Zephyr Antique Laid paper, which was manufactured, acid-free, in Saint-Jérôme, Quebec, from second-growth forests. This book was printed with vegetable-based ink on a 1965 Heidelberg KORD offset litho press. Its pages were folded on a Baumfolder, gathered by hand, bound on a Sulby Auto-Minabinda and trimmed on a Polar single-knife cutter.

Edited for the press by Nicole Markotić
Designed by Alana Wilcox
Cover photograph of Betty, a Rocky Mountain House hen,
    by Graham Law (glaw.com), courtesy of the photographer

Coach House Books
80 bpNichol Lane
Toronto ON M5S 3J4
Canada

416 979 2217
800 367 6360

mail@chbooks.com
www.chbooks.com